Fun to do

PRESENTS

Irene Newington

CONTENTS

Swallow

What You Will Need

Before you begin to make your presents it is a good idea to get ready a few useful tools. You will need a pencil, eraser and ruler for drawing and marking out; and paint or felt-tip pens for decorating. You can use a pair of round-ended scissors for cutting paper and thin card, but you will need to ask a grown up to cut thick card for you with a craft knife. You can use glue, staplers or tape for fixing things together, and you will need a needle and thread ready for sewing.

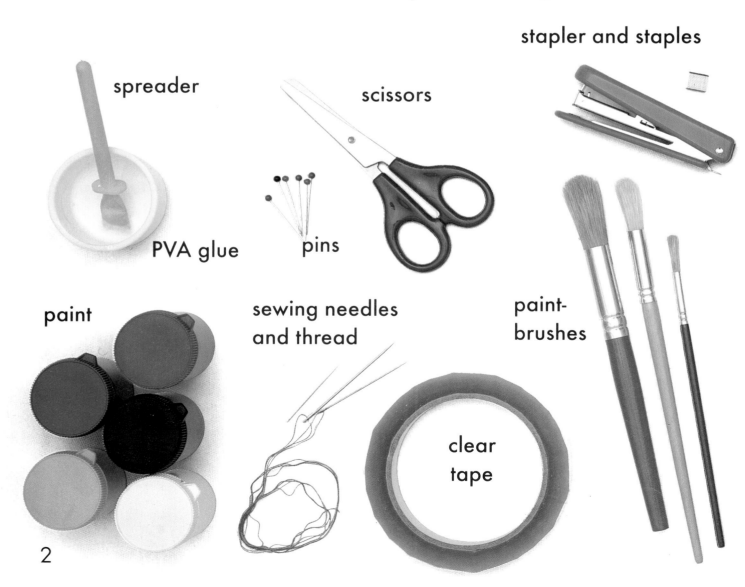

stapler and staples

spreader

scissors

PVA glue

pins

paint

sewing needles and thread

paint-brushes

clear tape

Other Useful Things

When you begin to make presents you will find that all sorts of things come in useful. Listed below are just a few. Collect useful odds and ends in a cardboard box and keep adding to your collection.

Cardboard tubes, yoghurt pots, bottle tops, jar lids, cereal packets, matchboxes, thick card, paper plates, sweet wrappers, tissue-paper, wrapping paper, colour magazines, felt, string, wool oddments, ribbon ends, lolly sticks, material off-cuts, cotton reels, corks, tinsel, pipe cleaners, sequins, glitter, straws, self-adhesive shapes, fir-cones, dried flowers, buttons and beads.

masking tape

tracing paper

thick card

craft knife

felt-tip pens

pencil sharpener

metal ruler

pencil and eraser

plastic ruler

Remember

☆ Wear an apron and cover the work area.
☆ Collect together the items in the materials box at the beginning of each project.
☆ Always ask an adult for help when you see this sign !
☆ Clear up after yourself.

Teddy Bear Pencil Holder

This jolly bear can be hung up on the wall or pinned onto a noticeboard.

Materials

felt

card

ribbon

1 Trace off the teddy bear templates on pages 30 and 31 onto a piece of card and cut out.

2 Use felt-tip pens to colour in the bear's eyes, nose and mouth. Staple the head to the body.

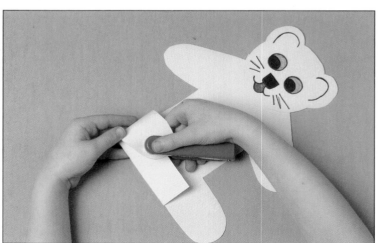

3 Fold up the flap of card at the bottom of the body. Fold the legs inwards over the flap. Staple each leg to the flap to make a pocket.

4 Fold the bear's arms inwards and staple together.

4

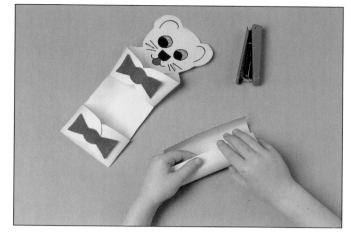

5 Cut 2 bows from the felt and glue over the staples.

6 Cut a piece of card 12 cm x 16 cm, roll up into a tube and staple in place.

7 Tape a ribbon loop to the back of the bear's head to hang it up with. Push the tube down between the paws.

To finish the present off slip some coloured pencils or felt-tip pens into the tube. For Hallowe'en make a black cat holder. For Easter make a rabbit holder and fill it with chocolate eggs.

Butterfly Card

An unusual card that is a present too.

Materials

ribbon, safety pin, sticky pad, thin card, foil tape, sequins, glitter, wrapping paper

1 Cut a piece of card 30 cm x 12 cm. Fold in half.

3 Draw round the outline of the butterfly with a black felt-tip pen. Decorate the body.

2 Trace off the butterfly template (page 30) onto the front of the card.

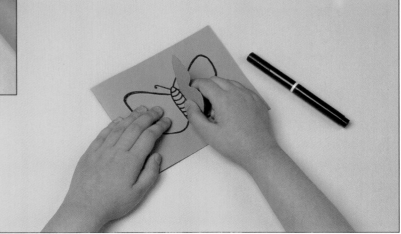

!4 Cut around the outside of the butterfly wings and lift up.

5 Cut a piece of card 13 cm x 10 cm. Cover both sides with wrapping paper.

6 Open up the card. Tape the covered piece of card in place behind the lifted butterfly.

7 Trace off the butterfly template onto a piece of card and cut out. Decorate the wings with sequins and glitter.

To finish off the card, lay a thin piece of ribbon along the folded edge and tie into a decorative bow on the outside.

8 Tape a small safety pin to the back of the butterfly and secure inside the card with a sticky pad.

Scented Clown

Materials

piece of fabric about 20cm square

pot-pourri

wool

4 small beads

1 large wooden bead

rubber band

ribbon

A colourful clown perfect for hanging in the wardrobe to keep clothes smelling sweet.

1 Sew a bead onto each corner of the piece of fabric.

3 Paint the large wooden bead white. When it is dry, draw on a clown's face with felt-tip pens.

4 Cut 12 pieces of wool each measuring about 5 cm. Tie into a bundle and secure with a knot.

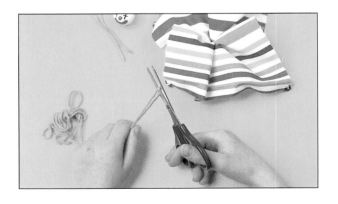

2 Put a heap of pot-pourri in the middle of the fabric. Gather up the edges to make a ball and fasten securely with the rubber band.

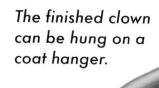

The finished clown can be hung on a coat hanger.

5 Thread wool onto a needle and sew a couple of stitches through the back of the wig.

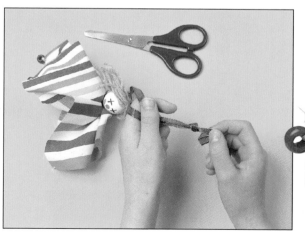

6 Now thread on the clown's head and sew securely onto the bag.

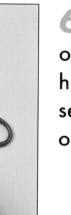

7 Thread a ribbon through the top of the clown's wig and knot the ends together.

Ollie Octopus

A perfect present for a friend to hang from the bedroom ceiling.

Materials

chunky wool

newspaper

string

joggle eyes

bits of felt

crêpe paper

elastic

card

1 Roll some newspaper into a ball and tape it into shape.

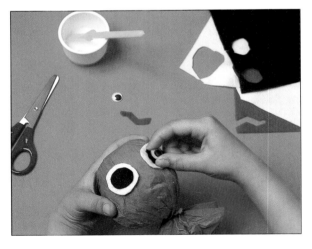

2 Cover the ball with crêpe paper. Tie a piece of string tightly around the neck, leaving a frill.

3 Glue 2 black felt circles onto 2 larger white felt circles and stick onto the ball. Stick the joggle eyes on top. Cut a zig zag mouth from red felt and glue on too.

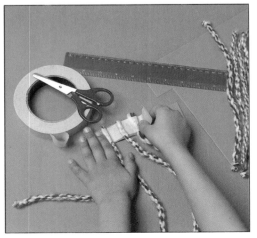

4 Cut 8 pieces of thick wool each 25 cm long. Tape these evenly along a strip of card 15 cm x 3 cm.

10

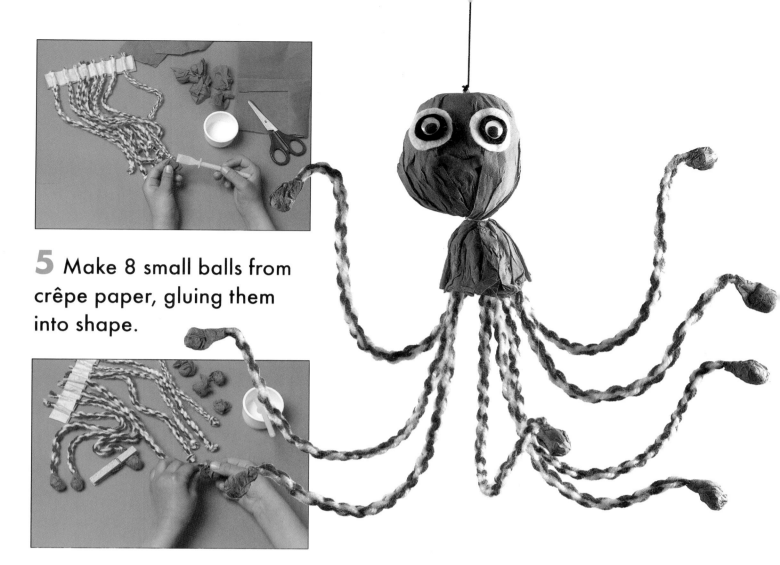

5 Make 8 small balls from crêpe paper, gluing them into shape.

6 Glue a ball to the bottom of each piece of wool.

7 Tape the card strip into a circle and glue it inside the frill of the neck.

Fasten a piece of elastic to Ollie's head so that he bounces up and down when he is hung up.

OTHER IDEAS

For a Hallowe'en gift
Make a spider out of black paper and use pipe cleaners for the legs.
For a gift for a newborn baby
Use pastel colours and securely sew bells to the ends of the wool. Hang above the baby's cot well out of reach.

Materials

wrapping paper

strips of crêpe paper

washing-up liquid bottle

box

6 garden sticks

coloured card

Ringo

Make this game for a brother or sister, then play it together to see who can get the best score.

1 Choose a wrapping paper with a repeat pattern and cut out 6 figures from it. Glue these onto thin card and cut around the outline.

2 Tape each figure to the top of a garden stick.

3 Cover the box with wrapping paper.

! **4** Poke 6 holes through the top of the box, spacing them out evenly.

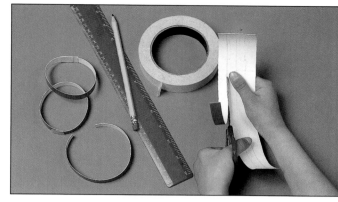

5 Use a coin or small bottle lid to draw out 6 circles from coloured card. Cut out and number them 1 to 6. Glue a number next to each hole.

6 Cut open a washing-up liquid bottle. Cut 6 1-cm strips from the plastic. Tape the strips into rings.

7 Wind the strips of crêpe paper around the rings until the plastic is completely covered. Secure the ends of the paper with tape.

Push the sticks into the holes. Take it in turns to see how many figures you can ring. The first one to reach 50 is the winner.

13

Wizard Birthday Badge

Make this super badge for a friend to wear on his or her birthday.

1 Mark in a face on the head of the peg with felt-tip pens.

2 Cut a piece of black felt 15 cm x 9 cm. Sew a line of running stitches up one long edge, leaving about 10 cm of thread at each end.

3 Pull both ends of the thread to gather up the felt. Put the dress around the peg's neck and tie securely at the back.

4 Cut 2 arms from white card and glue onto the dress. Cut a number (the age of your friend) from the gold card and stick onto the front of the dress.

5 Cut a piece of purple felt 8 cm x 8 cm and sew a line of running stitches along one edge.   Gather the stitches.

6 Put the cloak over the dress and tie securely at the front of the wizard's neck. Decorate with stars.

7 Cut a circle of blue card and fold into 4. Cut along one fold line to the middle. Put glue along one cut edge and slide under the other to make a cone shape. Decorate with stars.

8 Glue some cotton-wool onto the head for the hair and a beard and stick the hat on top. Attach a safety pin to the back of the cloak.

For Hallowe'en make a peg doll witch and give her a broom to hold.

15

Elephant Memo Clip

The perfect present for a busy parent.

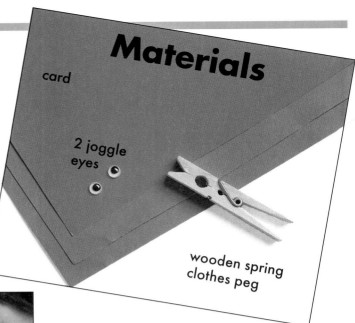

Materials

card

2 joggle eyes

wooden spring clothes peg

1 Trace off the elephant templates on page 31 onto stiff card. You will need 2 bodies, 2 ears and 1 trunk.

2 Cut out and decorate with paint and felt-tip pens.

3 Glue the peg between the front and back of the elephant's body so that it sticks out at the top by about 1cm. Leave to dry.

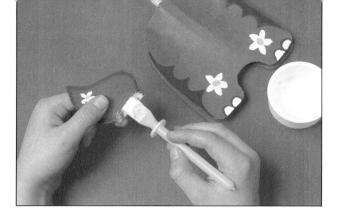

4 Glue the ears behind the front of the body. Leave to dry.

6 Stick on the joggle eyes. Draw and cut out 2 tusks from white card. Glue these on either side of the trunk.

5 Make a fold down the middle of the trunk. Glue onto the centre of the elephant's face.

If you use a bulldog clip instead of a peg, the memo clip can be hung on a pin. You can vary the design too.

Funny Face Kite

Make 2 of these and fly them with a friend.

1 Cut 2 strips of card measuring 26 cm x 2 cm and 17 cm x 2 cm. Staple into a cross. Glue the card cross onto a large piece of crêpe paper and leave to dry.

Materials

coloured tissue-paper

thick card

thin white paper

crêpe paper

string

3 To strengthen the cross stick pieces of masking tape over it.

4 Cut out and colour 2 eyes, a nose and a mouth. Stick onto the front of the kite.

2 Mark a line across each corner of the paper about 1 cm from the card cross. Cut along these lines. Fold over the edge of paper all the way round and glue down.

18

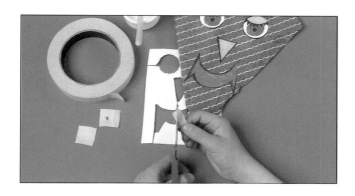

5 Fold a piece of masking tape into a square and cut a hole in the centre of it. Make 3. Tape the squares to the side and bottom corners of the kite.

6 Cover the back of the kite with a piece of crêpe paper cut to fit and glued in place.

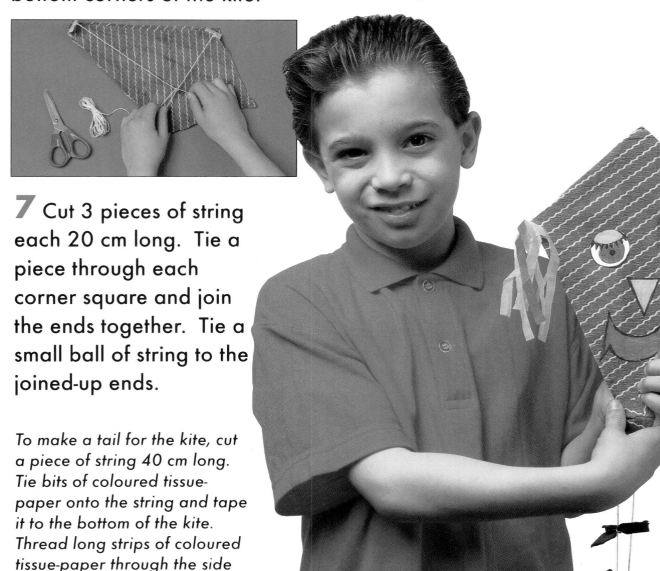

7 Cut 3 pieces of string each 20 cm long. Tie a piece through each corner square and join the ends together. Tie a small ball of string to the joined-up ends.

To make a tail for the kite, cut a piece of string 40 cm long. Tie bits of coloured tissue-paper onto the string and tape it to the bottom of the kite. Thread long strips of coloured tissue-paper through the side holes to make tassels.

19

Photo Frame

Put a picture of yourself in this present and give it to your grandparents.

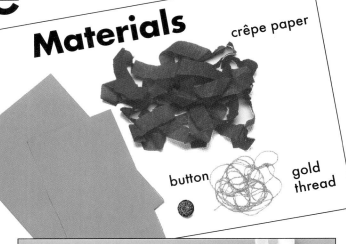

Materials

crêpe paper

thick card

button   gold thread

1 Cut out 2 pieces of card each measuring 20 cm x 16 cm. Draw a line as wide as your ruler all the way round one piece of card. Cut out the middle space.

2 Wind 2-cm wide strips of crêpe paper around the cardboard frame, fixing in place with a dab of glue here and there.

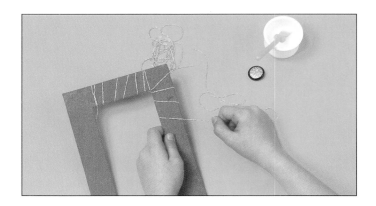

3 Tie the gold thread to the frame and wrap it round and round. Secure the thread with a knot at the back.

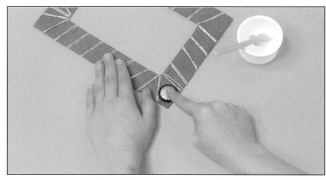

4 Glue a large button to one corner.

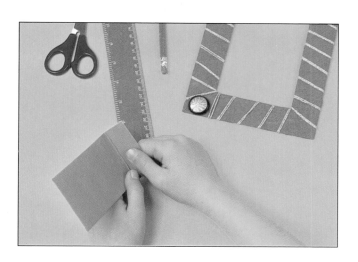

5 Cut out a piece of card measuring 13 cm x 6 cm. Draw a line 2 cm in from the edge. Score along the line and gently bend back.

6 Glue the support arm onto the back card 10 cm up from the bottom edge and secure with masking tape. Leave under a weight to dry.

7 Put glue along 3 sides of the back card leaving the top edge unglued. Press the covered frame onto it and leave under a weight to dry.

When the glue has dried, you can slip a photo of yourself into the frame.

21

Flower Cart

The perfect present for Mother's Day.

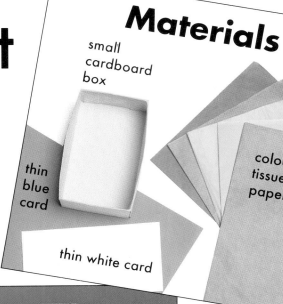

Materials

small cardboard box

thin blue card

thin white card

coloured tissue-paper

1 Put the box on a sheet of tissue-paper. Push the paper over the edges of the box and secure with glue.

2 Cut a strip of blue card 18 cm x 2 cm. Decorate with felt-tip pens.

3 Staple the decorated strip of card to the box to make a handle.

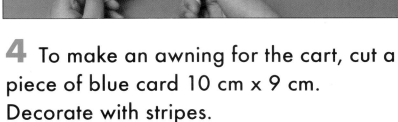

4 To make an awning for the cart, cut a piece of blue card 10 cm x 9 cm. Decorate with stripes.

5 Fold the card in half and staple to the handle.

6 Use a yoghurt carton to draw out 2 circles onto white card. Cut out. Draw in the spokes and staple to either side of the cart.

The flower cart, brimming with tissue-paper flowers, will make a beautiful table or windowsill decoration.

7 Crumple up some green tissue-paper and fill the cart with it. Cut out flower shapes from coloured tissue-paper and glue onto the green base. Stick small balls of coloured tissue-paper in the centre of the flower shapes.

Eggs in a Basket

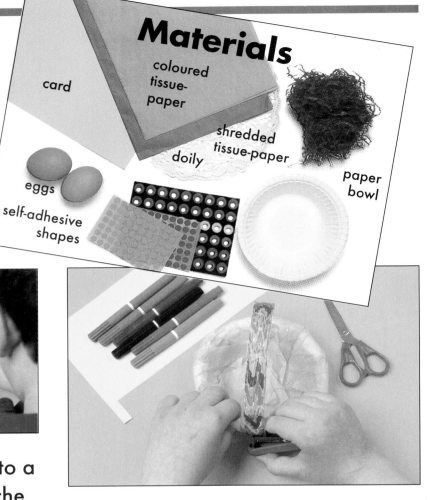

Materials
card · coloured tissue-paper · shredded tissue-paper · doily · eggs · self-adhesive shapes · paper bowl

A colourful surprise for Easter Day!

1 Place the paper bowl onto a piece of tissue-paper. Pull the paper over the edges of the bowl and smooth down.

3 Glue a thin strip of blue tissue-paper around the bowl. Stick bits cut from the doily to the rim of the bowl. Fill with shredded tissue-paper.

2 For a handle, cut a strip of card, decorate and staple to the bowl.

4 Make a hole at the top of an egg with a darning needle. Make a larger hole at the bottom.

5 Hold the egg over a bowl and blow through the smaller hole until the egg is empty. Carefully rinse and drain the egg.

6 When the egg is dry cover the holes with masking tape. Paint the egg all over.

Place the decorated eggs in the basket on a nest of shredded tissue-paper. Scatter small sugar or chocolate eggs all around. You could make a gift tag from card and tie it on to the handle.

7 When the paint is dry, decorate the egg with self-adhesive shapes.

25

Egg and Chick Mobile

Make this beautiful springtime gift.

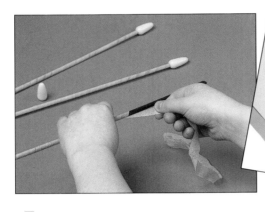

Materials

yellow and white card

yellow cotton-wool balls

strips of crêpe paper

3 garden sticks

string

ribbon

8 joggle eyes

7 beads

gold thread

1 Wrap strips of crêpe paper round the garden sticks and push a bead onto each end.

! **2** Make a star shape out of the decorated sticks. Tie in the middle with the string.

3 Draw 4 chick and 8 wing shapes onto yellow card using the templates on page 30. Cut out.

4 Glue yellow cotton-wool balls, wings and joggle eyes onto both sides of each chick.

26

5 Draw 4 egg shapes (template on page 30) onto white card. Cut out.

6 Use felt-tip pens to decorate the eggs on both sides.

!7 Pierce holes through the eggs and chicks. Tie gold thread through each hole. Knot the ends and loop onto the star.

Thread a bead onto a ribbon and fasten to the centre of the star. Hang up your mobile.

A CHRISTMAS VARIATION
Cut out 3 trees, 3 snowmen and 1 star from white card and decorate. Use gold thread to tie the trees and snowmen to each arm of the mobile and hang the star from the middle.

Mini Felt Stockings

The perfect present for the Christmas tree.

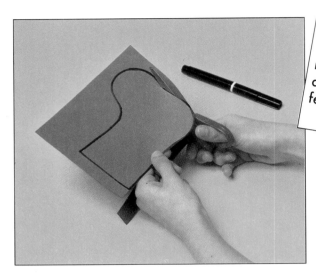

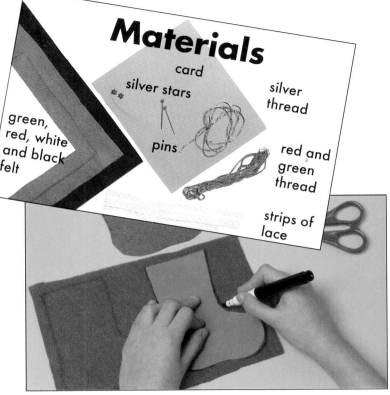

Materials

card

silver stars

silver thread

green, red, white and black felt

pins

red and green thread

strips of lace

1 Trace off the stocking on page 31 onto card and cut out to make a template.

2 Draw round the stocking template twice on the red felt and twice on the green felt. Cut out. Pin the red stockings together and the green stockings together.

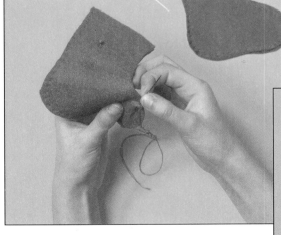

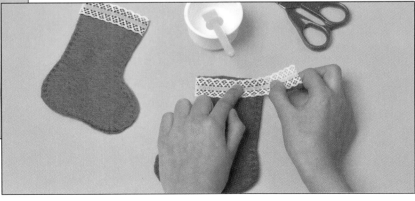

3 Sew an even line of running stitches around the stockings, leaving the tops open.

4 Cut 2 small pieces of lace to fit around the top of the stockings. Glue in place.

5 Cut 2 snowmen from white felt (template on page 31) and glue to the stockings. Mark faces and buttons with felt-tip pen.

6 Cut 2 hats from black felt (template page 31) and glue in place. Stick a silver star above the snowmen.

7 Sew a loop of silver thread through the top of each stocking. They can be hung from a tree and filled with small presents.

Make several stockings, one for each member of your family, and decorate each with a different Christmas design.

29

Templates

It is a good idea to make a card template that you can re-use time and time again. Lay a piece of tracing paper over the required template. Draw around the outline with a pencil. Turn over the tracing paper and scribble over the pencil outline. Turn the tracing paper over once again and lay down onto a piece of thick card. Carefully draw around the pencil outline. Remove the tracing paper. The outline of the traced shape on the card may be quite faint. Go over it with black felt-tip pen. Cut out and label the card template and keep it in a safe place. Use the card template to draw around as many times as is needed onto paper, card or material.

Cat Pencil Holder
(alternative pages 4-5)
HEAD

Egg and
Chick Mobile
(pages 26-27)
WING

Teddy Bear Pencil
Holder
(pages 4-5)
HEAD

Egg and Chick Mobile
(pages 26-27)
CHICK

Egg and Chick Mobile
(pages 26-27)
EGG

Buttefly Card
(pages 6-7)
BUTTERFLY

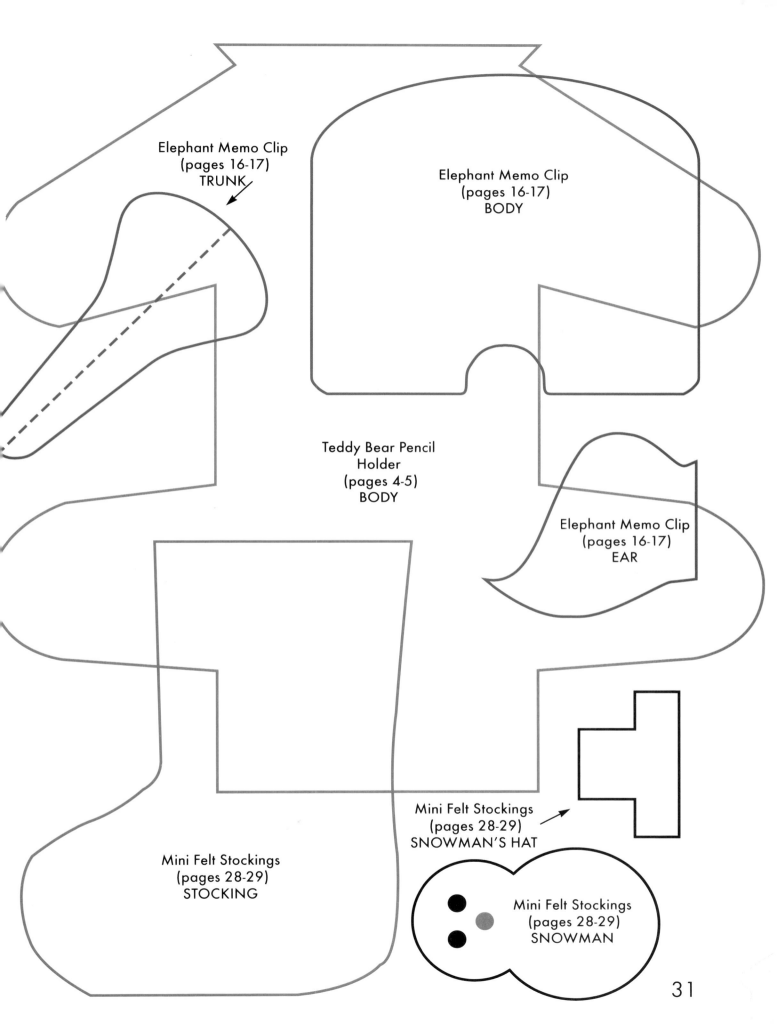

Elephant Memo Clip
(pages 16-17)
TRUNK

Elephant Memo Clip
(pages 16-17)
BODY

Teddy Bear Pencil
Holder
(pages 4-5)
BODY

Elephant Memo Clip
(pages 16-17)
EAR

Mini Felt Stockings
(pages 28-29)
STOCKING

Mini Felt Stockings
(pages 28-29)
SNOWMAN'S HAT

Mini Felt Stockings
(pages 28-29)
SNOWMAN

Advice to Parents

Children love to give presents, especially those that they have made themselves. In this book a wide selection of present ideas has been given so that your child can make gifts suitable for any member of the family for many special occasions, including birthdays, Mother's Day, Father's Day, Easter and Christmas. The information on this page is designed to help you to encourage your child to begin present-making.

Tools

Paint From a small selection of paints – red, yellow, blue, black and white – all other colours can be obtained by mixing. Encourage your child to explore colour mixing for herself. Buy ready-mixed water-based paint in the economy washing-up liquid bottle size. Always ensure that paint has dried before going on to the next step in the project.

Felt-tip Pens A good set of felt-tip pens is also a good idea for decorating presents. They have the advantage over paints because the child will not have to wait for them to dry.

Glue Solvent-free PVA adhesive is recommended as it is versatile, clean, strong and safe.

Scissors For the sake of safety children should use small scissors with round-ended metal blades and plastic handles. Although these are fine for cutting paper and thin card, they will not cut thick card and this is best done by you. This will often require a craft knife. Use a metal ruler to provide a straight cutting edge. If you do not have a cutting mat, use an old chopping board or very thick card to protect the work surface beneath.

Paper and Card Try to keep both white and coloured paper in the house. Do recycle paper whenever possible. Make use of off-cuts of wallpaper lining paper for example. Coloured card can be expensive: old cereal packets, folded flat, are perfect when a thin to medium-weight card is needed. Simply paint the unprinted side of the card whatever colour is required.

Materials

Odds and Ends Box None of the presents in this book requires you to buy expensive materials. Almost all can be made with things that can be found around the home: food packets, bits of fabric, wool oddments, etc. In preparation for present-making, and so that you do not have to turn the house upside down every time your child gets the present-making urge, do encourage your child to collect useful things and provide them with a box for that purpose. Refer to page 3 for a list of things to collect.

Joggle Eyes These can be bought from craft or needlework shops. They are not expensive.

Wooden Dolly Pegs These can be bought very cheaply from hardware shops.

Useful Tips

• Always put a piece of tape over staples for safety.
• When gluing together two bits of card, use a paper-clip to hold them in place.
• Keep a template in place with a paper-clip or a piece of tape.
• To make a neat hole in a piece of card, lay the card over a flattened ball of play dough or modelling clay and pierce with a sharp pencil or knitting needle.
• A bradawl is also useful for making neat holes through thick or decorated card.
• When your child is cutting around a shape, he or she will find it easier to roughly trim off the excess paper or card first before neatly cutting around the outline.

Finishing Off

Making Wrapping Paper It can be just as much fun wrapping the presents as making them up. As wrapping paper is very expensive, it's a good idea to encourage children to make their own. One of the simplest ways to make wrapping paper is to print or stencil a repeat pattern onto a sheet of paper.

• A Potato Print Paper: Cut a potato in half. Cut a simple shape, a cross for example, from one half of the potato. Lay out some paint on to a plate and dip the potato into it. Print with the painted potato on to a large sheet of paper. As the print begins to fade, dip the potato in paint again.

• A Stencilled Paper: Fold a small piece of card in half. Draw half of a symmetrical shape along the fold line, a heart, butterfly, flower, tree, or even a person for example. Open out the stencil and lay it onto a large piece of paper. Dab a brushful of paint over the stencil, taking care not to go under the edges. Carefully lift up the stencil and reposition on the paper. Build up a random pattern of stencilled pictures across the paper.

Making a Gift Tag Fold a small piece of card in half. Decorate the card with felt-tip pens and write a greeting inside. Make a hole in the corner of the card, thread through a thin ribbon, and tie onto the gift.

Wrapping Bulky Gifts Save shoe boxes for wrapping odd-shaped presents. The box can be wrapped in homemade wrapping paper. Make a protective nest in the box by shredding up bits of coloured paper or tissue-paper. Wind a ribbon around the box for an extra special finish. The ends of the ribbon can be attractively curled by pulling closed scissors blades along them.

Swallow is an imprint of Merehurst Limited
Reprinted 1996 by Merehurst Limited
Ferry House, 51-57 Lacy Road, Putney, London SW15 1PR

© Copyright 1993 Merehurst Limited
ISBN 1 898018 15 4

All rights reserved.

A catalogue record for this book is available from the British Library.

Project Editor: Cheryl Brown
Designer: Anita Ruddell
Photography by Jon Bouchier
Colour separation by Scantrans Pte Limited, Singapore
Printed in Italy by G. Canale & C., S.p.A.

The publisher would like to thank the staff and children of Riversdale Primary School, London Borough of Wandsworth, The Early Learning Centre, Joseph Mills-Brown, Rand Hashim and Jay Darlington for their help in producing the photographs for this book.